Hold a problem in
your mind

Open this book to
any page

And there will be
your answer

A Guide for the Advanced Soul

How to use this Guide

You have a problem or need guidance to help you make a decision. Picture this clearly in your mind; meditate on it so that the mind gradually subsides into stillness. This allows you to draw on your subconscious and intuitive powers to respond. Now put forward your request while randomly opening the book. The first words you read will tell you what you most need to hear.

Clearly it is your interpretation of the quotation that will give you your answer. Be open to what you read: interpreting it objectively, and without projecting your wishes on the outcome. The value of the reading will depend on how far you are willing to change in the direction indicated. Opposing the forces controlling your life creates disharmony around you.

Knowing that you create your personal reality is important, because this enables you to understand that all circumstances, events and experiences in the world flow from the centre of your being to provide a living feedback.

At this instant, you are a reflection of the universe, where all things and events exist simultaneously - the past, present, and the future juxtaposed. You contain all the potentialities of the whole world within you.

Your guidance is here for you to work with, from the point of your own reality.

A Guide for the Advanced Soul

CREATED & HANDWRITTEN BY
SUSAN HAYWARD

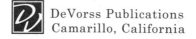
DeVorss Publications
Camarillo, California

A Guide for the Advanced Soul
Copyright © 1984, 2008 by Susan Hayward

First published by IN-TUNE BOOKS Australia in 1985
Text calligraphy: Susan Hayward, Liz Faul
Cover calligraphy: Margo Snape

ISBN: 9780875168395
Library of Congress Control Number: 2008933042
First DeVorss Publications edition, 2008
Second Printing, 2009

DeVorss & Company, Publisher
P.O. Box 1389
Camarillo CA 93011-1389
www.devorss.com

Printed in the United States of America

PREFACE TO THIS NEW EDITION

It has been 20 years since I first published A GUIDE FOR THE ADVANCED SOUL. I have been quite astounded, and very moved, by the way the book has touched the lives of so many people. It has become a trusted companion for many, and I have received hundreds of letters from readers, with many wonderful stories of their magical experiences of divination. I appreciate this feedback, and it encourages me to continue to produce inspirational books.

My vision back in 1984 was to create a handbook of positive and uplifting thoughts that would inspire anyone in need of guidance. I had begun to embrace the idea of synchronicity, and the concept that your subconscious can interpret simple messages from your environment into insight. Having discovered this principle of divination, my aim was to produce a book of simple truths from many different philosophies to help the reader focus on their Inner Voice.

What I am grateful for now is how the process of bringing my vision to life has advanced my own growth. The first manuscript of *The Guide* was, in fact, rejected by every publisher I approached. It therefore took a great deal of faith to maintain enough enthusiasm to continue.

The subsequent decision to self-publish *The Guide* was rather a challenging one, as I had no experience in graphic art or book production, nor any business background. In retrospect, I think it is a testament to the power of the inspirational messages of the book: they truly inspired me with the optimism to keep going.

I had fun producing this new edition because I was able to review quotes that no longer had impact for me, and also add new quotes which reflect my ongoing, eclectic appreciation of truth. In the course of my work, I have come to recognise again certain strong themes that run throughout *The Guide*: reminders to let go, to have faith, to just Be, and to remember to laugh and enjoy life.

I feel very honoured to have produced a book that has influenced others' lives. It inspires me to know that many people are today working on themselves and care deeply about perfecting their souls. I am grateful, along with my readers I am sure, for the teachings of the great spirits included in this anthology. The illumination these words have shone on our respective paths has been a guide to many advanced souls. May you also continue to be blessed by the spirit of these words.

Susan Hayward

A Letter to You

Dear Friend:

I have created this book for you to consult when you are faced with problems. It is a collection of beautiful words of wisdom that will guide and inspire you.

See yourself as part of the never-ending cycle of change in the universe and this book will reflect that change for you. Everything in the universe is continuously integrating and disintegrating- this produces transformation and growth. Your problems are caused by your resistance towards this natural cyclic movement of life.

When you randomly open this Guide you are addressing the universe, and it responds to your question, which you then interpret intuitively. Regard your problems as opportunities for learning and creating something new, and you will feel a sense of well-being that results from your shift in consciousness. Know that we are only presented with lessons when we are ready to learn them.

Above all, trust your own direction. I hope this Guide gives you confidence to follow your path and surrender to the inner intuitive voice that recognises the harmony and wholeness that has always been there.

I hope also that this contributes to the increasing new awareness and social transformation taking place throughout the world, that will unite all human beings as One.

Love,
  Susan

Be at peace
and see
a clear pattern and plan
running through
all your lives.

Nothing is by chance.

EILEEN CADDY
Footprints on the Path

You know quite well,
deep within you,
that there is only
a single magic,
a single power,
a single salvation...
and that is called loving.
Well then,
love your suffering.
Do not resist it, do not flee from it
It is only your aversion that hurts,
nothing else.

HERMAN HESSE

Do not take life's experiences
too seriously. Above all, do not
let them hurt you, for in reality
they are nothing but
dream experiences....

If circumstances are bad
and you have to bear them,
do not make them
a part of yourself.

Play your part in life,
but never forget that
it is only a role.

PARAMAHANSA YOGANANDA
Par-a-gram

Be willing to have it so;
acceptance of what
has happened is the
first step to overcoming the
consequences of any misfortune.

WILLIAM JAMES

... as the springs return -
regardless of time or man -
so is HOPE!
Sometimes but a tiny bud
has to push up
through the hard shell
of circumstance
to reach the light
of accomplishment.
Do not give up HOPE!

DOROTHY MILLER COLE

There is only one courage
and that is the courage
to go on dying to the past,
not to collect it,
not to accumulate it,
not to cling to it.

We all cling to the past,
and because we cling
to the past we become
unavailable
to the present.

BHAGWAN SHREE RAJNEESH
Walking in Zen, Sitting in Zen

Confine yourself
to
the
present.

MARCUS AURELIUS

Life is the movie you see through
your own unique eyes.

It makes little difference
what's happening out there.

Its how you take it that counts.

DENIS WAITLEY
The Winner's Edge

Who looks outside
dreams;
who looks inside
wakes.

C. G. JUNG

When you feel
    that you have reached the end
and that you cannot go
                one step further,
    when life seems to be
    drained of all purpose:

What a wonderful opportunity
    to start all over again,
        to turn over a new page.

EILEEN CADDY
Footprints on the Path

Every now and then go away,
  have a little relaxation,
  for when you come back
  to your work
  your judgement will be surer;
  since to remain constantly at work
  will cause you to lose power
                of judgement ...

Go some distance away
  because the work appears smaller
  and more of it
  can be taken in at a glance,
  and a lack of harmony
  or proportion
            is more readily seen.

LEONARDO DA VINCI

Don't try to force anything.
Let life be a deep let-go.

See God opening millions
of flowers every day
without forcing
the buds.

BHAGWAN SHREE RAJNEESH
Dying for Enlightenment

Stop sitting there
    with your hands folded
    looking on, doing nothing;

Get into action
    and live this full
            and glorious life.

Now.

You have to do it.

EILEEN CADDY
The Dawn of Change

Only in relationship can you
know yourself, not in abstraction
and certainly not in isolation.

The movement of behaviour
is the sure guide to yourself, it's
the mirror of your consciousness;
this mirror will reveal its content,
the images, the attachments, the
fears, the loneliness, the joy and
sorrow.

Poverty lies in running away
from this, either in its
sublimations or its identities.

J. KRISHNAMURTI

Everyone
and everything
around you
is your
teacher.

KEN KEYES, JR
Handbook to Higher Consciousness

Thoughts are things;
they have tremendous power.

Thoughts of doubt and fear
are pathways to failure.
When you conquer negative attitudes
of doubt and fear you conquer failure.

Thoughts crystallize into habit
and habit solidifies into circumstance.

BRIAN ADAMS
How to Succeed

Everything that happens and
everything that befalls us
has a meaning,
    but it is often difficult to
    recognize it.

Also in the book of life
    every page has two sides:
we human beings fill the
upper side with our plans,
hopes and wishes,
but Providence writes on the
other side, and what it ordains
    is seldom our goal.

NISÂMÎ

Inner peace
can be reached
only when we practice
forgiveness.

Forgiveness
is the letting go of the past,
and is therefore
the means for correcting
our misperceptions.

GERALD G. JAMPOLSKY
Love is Letting Go of Fear

If you attack apparent negativity
with negativity,
you merely feed
and inflame the source.

It's always best
to take the positive
in any conflict.

If you genuinely love,
or at least
send kind thoughts
to a thing,
it will change
before your eyes.

JOHN & LYN ST. CLAIR THOMAS
Eyes of the Beholder

)(

Man cannot discover new oceans
until he has courage
to lose sight
of the shore.

UNKNOWN

Life is like a wild tiger.
You can either lie down
                    and let it
Lay its paw on your head -
Or sit on its back and ride it.

RIDE THE WILD TIGER

One may not
        reach the dawn
save by
    the path
        of the night.

KAHLIL GIBRAN
Sand and Foam

Have no fear
   of moving into the unknown.
Simply step out fearlessly
   knowing that I am with you,
   therefore no harm can befall you;
   all is very very well.

Do this in complete faith
   and confidence.

EILEEN CADDY
Footprints on the Path

How wonderful is the way
in which, with quite ordinary folk,
power leaps to our aid
in any time of emergency.
We lead timid lives,
shrinking from difficult tasks
till perhaps we are forced into them
or ourselves determine on them,
and immediately we seem to
unlock the unseen forces.
When we have to face danger,
then courage comes,
when trial puts a long-continued
strain upon us, we find ourselves
possessed by the power to endure;

if when disaster ultimately brings
the fall which we so long dreaded,
we feel underneath us the strength
as of the everlasting arms.
Common experience teaches that
when great demands are made upon us,
if only we fearlessly accept
the challenge and confidently
expend our strength,
every danger or difficulty
brings its own strength -
"As thy days so shall thy strength be."

J. A. HADFIELD
The Psychology of Power

Most people don't know
    how brave they really are.

In fact, many potential heroes
    both men and women
live out their lives in self-doubt.

If they only knew
    they had these deep resources,
it would help give them the self-reliance
    to meet most problems,
        even a big crisis.

R.E. CHAMBERS

The first rule is
to keep an untroubled spirit.

The second is
look things in the face
and
know them for what they are.

MARCUS AURELIUS
Meditations

You must begin
to trust yourself.

If you do not
then you will forever
be looking to others
to prove your own merit to you,
and you will never be satisfied.

You will always be asking
others what to do,
and at the same time
resenting those
from whom
you seek such aid.

JANE ROBERTS
The Nature of Personal Reality

Come to the edge, he said.
They said: We are afraid.
Come to the edge, he said.
They came.
He pushed them...and they flew.

GUILLAUME APOLLINAIRE

Why destroy
   your present happiness
      by a distant misery,
         which may never
            come at all ?

For every substantial grief
   has twenty shadows
      and most of the shadows
         are of your own making.

SYDNEY SMITH

Be open to your
happiness
and sadness
as they arise.

JOHN & LYN ST·CLAIR THOMAS
Eyes of the Beholder

*Life is either
    a daring adventure
        or nothing.*

HELEN KELLER

We are not here just to survive
and live long...
We are here to live and know life
in its multi-dimensions
to know life in its richness,
in all its variety.

And when a man lives
multi-dimensionally,
explores all possibilities available,
never shrinks back from any challenge,
goes, rushes to it, welcomes it,
rises to the occasion
then life becomes a flame,
life blooms.

BHAGWAN SHREE RAJNEESH
The Sacred Yes

Until one is committed, there is hesitancy, the chance to draw back, always ineffectiveness. Concerning all acts of initiative (and creation), there is one elementary truth, the ignorance of which kills countless ideas and splendid plans: that the moment one definitely commits oneself, then Providence moves too.

All sorts of things occur to help one that would never otherwise have occurred. A whole stream of events issues from the decision, raising in one's favour all manner of unforeseen incidents and meetings and material assistance, which no man could have dreamed would have come his way.

Whatever you can do
or dream you can,
begin it.

Boldness has genius, magic
and power in it.

Begin it now.

GOETHE

Ask, and it shall be given you;
seek, and ye shall find;
knock, and it shall be opened
unto you.

For every one that asketh,
receiveth;
and he that seeketh,
findeth;
and to him that knocketh
it shall be opened.

MATTHEW 7:7,8

Expect your every need
to be met,
expect the answer
to every problem,
expect abundance
on every level,
expect to grow spiritually.

EILEEN CADDY
The Dawn of Change

Expect the best;
   convert problems into opportunities;
Be dissatisfied with the status quo;
Focus on where you want to go,
   instead of where you're coming from;
and most importantly,
   Decide to be happy,
      knowing it's an attitude,
   a habit gained from daily practise,
      and not a result or payoff.

DENIS WAITLEY
The Winner's Edge

God continually showers the
fullness of his grace
on every being in the universe,
but we consent to receive it
to a greater
or lesser extent.

In purely spiritual matters,
God grants all desires.

Those who have less
have asked for less.

SIMONE WEIL
Waiting for God

If we could read the secret history
of our enemies,

we would find in each man's life
a sorrow and a suffering
enough to disarm all hostility.

HENRY WADSWORTH LONGFELLOW

We cannot live only for ourselves.
A thousand fibers connect us
with our fellow men;
and among those fibers,
as sympathetic threads,
our actions run as causes,
and they come back to us
as effects.

HERMAN MELVILLE

Let there be more
   joy and laughter
      in your living.

EILEEN CADDY
God Spoke to Me

Every moment of your life
is infinitely creative
and the universe
is endlessly bountiful.

Just put forth
a clear enough request,
and everything
your heart desires
must come to you.

SHAKTI GAWAIN
Creative Visualisation

The fastest way
to freedom
is to
feel
your feelings.

GITA BELLIN

Be aware of the reality of your feelings. As you become more aware of your beliefs over a period of time, you will see how they bring forth certain feelings automatically.

A man who is sure of himself is <u>not</u> angry at every slight done him, nor does he carry grudges. A man who fears for his own worth, however, <u>is</u> furious under such conditions.

The free flow of your emotions will always lead you back to your conscious beliefs if you do not impede them.

JANE ROBERTS
The Nature of Personal Reality

Disillusionment
with yourself
must precede
Enlightenment.

VERNON HOWARD
The Mystic Path to Cosmic Power

Learn your lessons
                quickly,

and move on.

EILEEN CADDY
The Dawn of Change

When you are inspired by
some great purpose,
some extraordinary project,
all your thoughts break their bonds;
your mind transcends limitations,
your consciousness expands
in every direction,
and you find yourself in a new,
great and wonderful world.
Dormant forces, faculties and talents
become alive, and you discover yourself
to be a greater person by far
than you ever dreamed
yourself to be.

PATANJALI

It is in
self-limitation

that a master
first shows himself.

J.W. VON GOETHE

Be like a very small
            joyous child
living gloriously in the
            ever present Now
without a single worry or concern
    about even the next
        moment of time.

EILEEN CADDY
The Dawn of Change

Go confidently
in the direction of your dreams!
Live the life you've imagined.

As you simplify your life,
the laws of the universe
will be simpler;
solitude will not be solitude,
poverty will not be poverty,
nor weakness weakness.

HENRY DAVID THOREAU

When love beckons to you, follow him,
 Though his ways are hard and steep
And when his wings enfold you,
                  yield to him,
   Though the sword hidden
among his pinions may wound you.

And when he speaks to you,
  believe in him,
Though his voice may shatter your dream
    as the north wind
      lays waste the garden.

KAHLIL GIBRAN
The Prophet

The course of human life is
like that of a great river which, by
the force of its own swiftness, takes
quite new and unforeseen channels
where before there was no current—
such varied currents and unpremedi-
tated changes are part of God's
purpose for our lives.

Life is not an artificial canal
to be confined within prescribed
channels.

When once this is clearly seen
in our own lives, then we shall not
be able to be misled by any mere
fabrications.

RABINDRANATH TAGORE

Thoughts
are like
boomerangs.

EILEEN CADDY
The Dawn of Change

The most powerful thing
you can do to change the world,
is to change your own beliefs
about the nature of life, people,
reality, to something
more positive...
and begin to act
accordingly.

SHAKTI GAWAIN
Creative Visualisation

Your pain
is the breaking
of the shell
that encloses
your understanding.

KAHLIL GIBRAN
The Prophet

Take heart,
   truth and happiness
      will get you in the end.

You can't lose in this game.

Have fun.

It goes on too long
   to be taken seriously
      all the time.

JOHN & LYN ST. CLAIR THOMAS
Eyes of the Beholder

Dwell not on the past.
Use it to illustrate a point,
then leave it behind.
Nothing really matters
except what you do now
in this instant of time.

From this moment onward
you can be an entirely different person,
filled with love and understanding,
ready with an outstretched hand,
uplifted and positive
in every thought
and deed.

EILEEN CADDY
God Spoke to Me

The only way to deal
with the future
is to function efficiently
in the Now.

GITA BELLIN

Life is a series
of natural
and spontaneous
changes.

Don't resist them -
that only creates sorrow.

Let reality be reality.

Let things flow naturally forward
in whatever way
they like.

LAO-TSE

The fates lead
him who will—

him who won't,
they drag.

SENECA

*I know I'm not seeing things
as they are,
I'm seeing things as I am.*

LAUREL LEE

One has just to be oneself.
That's my basic message.

The moment you accept yourself
as you are,
all burdens,
all mountainous burdens
simply disappear.

Then life is a sheer joy,
a festival of lights.

BHAGWAN SHREE RAJNEESH
The Sound of One Hand Clapping

A human being
is a single being.

Unique
and unrepeatable.

JOHN PAUL II

We are members
of a vast cosmic orchestra.
in which each living instrument
is essential to the
complementary and
harmonious
playing of
the
whole.

J. ALLEN BOONE
Kinship With All Life

Life is full
      and overflowing
            with the new.

But it is necessary to empty out
      the old to make room
            for the new to enter.

EILEEN CADDY
Footprints on the Path

Change
is never a loss –

it is change only.

VERNON HOWARD
The Mystic Path to Cosmic Power

Expand
in consciousness –
be ready to accept anything
now,
at any time.

EILEEN CADDY
God Spoke to Me

Trials are but lessons
that you failed to learn
presented once again,
so where you made a faulty choice before
you can now make a better one,
and thus escape all pain
that what you chose before
has brought to you.

A COURSE IN MIRACLES

You are given the gifts of the gods;
   you create your reality
   according to your beliefs.

Yours is the creative energy
   that makes your world.

There are no limitations
   to the self
   except those you believe in.

JANE ROBERTS
The Nature of Personal Reality

*If you know
you want it,
Have it.*

GITA BELLIN

The most effective way
to achieve right relations
with any living thing
is to look for the best in it,
and then help that best
into the fullest expression.

J. ALLEN BOONE
Kinship with All Life

The people
we are in relationship
with are always a mirror,
reflecting our own beliefs,
and simultaneously
we are mirrors,
reflecting their beliefs.

So relationship is one
of the most powerful tools for growth...
if we look honestly at our
relationships we can see so much
about how we
have created them.

SHAKTI GAWAIN
Creative Visualisation

Peace of mind
   comes from not wanting
      to change others,
         but by simply accepting them
            as they are.

True acceptance
   is always without demands
      and expectations.

GERALD G. JAMPOLSKY
Love is Letting Go of Fear

The snow goose
    need not bathe
        to make itself white.

        Neither need you
            do anything
                but be yourself.

LAO-TSE

To see your drama
clearly
is to be liberated
from it.

KEN KEYES, JR
Handbook to Higher Consciousness

*Everything
we do in life...*

Is it not just a game ?

GURURAJ ANANDA YOGI

For those who believe,
no proof is necessary.

For those who don't believe,
no proof is possible.

JOHN & LYN ST. CLAIR THOMA
Eyes of the Beholder

How much longer will you go on
   letting your energy sleep?

How much longer are you going
   to stay oblivious of the immensity
   of yourself?

Don't lose time in conflict;
   lose no time in doubt –
   time can never be recovered
   and if you miss an opportunity
   it may take many lives
   before another comes
   your way again.

BHAGWAN SHREE RAJNEESH
A Cup Of Tea

Seek always
for the answer within.

Be not influenced
by those around you,
by their thoughts
or their words.

EILEEN CADDY
God Spoke to Me

However many holy words
you read,
however many you speak,
What good will they do you
if you do not act upon them?

THE DHAMMAPADA

The more you depend
on forces
outside yourself,
the more you are dominated
by them.

HAROLD SHERMAN

We are what we think.
All that we are
      arises with our thoughts.
With our thoughts we make
   the world.

Speak or act with a pure mind
   and happiness will follow you
      as your shadow,
         unshakeable.

THE DHAMMAPADA

To every thing
there is a season,
and a time to every purpose
under the heaven.

ECCLESIASTES 3:1

Time is an invention.
Now is a reality.
So much creativity is happening
for the simple reason that we
have withdrawn ourselves
from past and future.

Our whole energy remains blocked
either in the past or in the future.

When you withdraw all your energy
from past and future a
tremendous explosion happens.

That explosion is creativity.

BHAGWAN SHREE RAJNEESH
The Goose Is Out

Until
 you can understand
  that nothing can happen to you,
 nothing can ever come to you
or be kept from you,
except in accord
 with your state
  of consciousness,
   you do not have
    the key to life.

PAUL TWITCHELL
The Flute of God
ECKANKAR

There is no separation
between us and God –
we are divine expressions
of the creative principle ...
there can be no real lack or scarcity;
there is nothing we have to try
to achieve or attract;
we contain the potential
for everything
within us.

SHAKTI GAWAIN
Creative Visualisation

To change one's life :

    Start immediately
    Do it flamboyantly
    No exceptions
        (no excuses)

WILLIAM JAMES

Each man has his own vocation.
The talent is the call.

There is one direction in which
all space is open to him. He has
faculties silently inviting him
thither to endless exertion.

He is like a ship in a river;
he runs against obstructions
on every side but one;
on that side all obstruction is
taken away, and he sweeps
serenely over a deepening channel
into an infinite sea.

RALPH WALDO EMERSON
Spiritual Laws

Life's fulfillment finds constant
contradictions in its path; but
those are necessary for the sake of
its advance.

The stream is saved from the
sluggishness of its current by the
perpetual opposition of the soil
through which it must cut its way.
It is the soil which forms its banks.

The Spirit of fight belongs to
the genius of life.

RABINDRANATH TAGORE

Be realistic:

Plan for a miracle.

BHAGWAN SHREE RAJNEESH

The impossible is possible
when people align with you.

When you do things with people,
not against them,
the amazing resources
of the Higher Self within
are mobilised.

GITA BELLIN

Great spirits
    have always encountered
        violent opposition
            from mediocre minds.

ALBERT EINSTEIN

A loving
  person lives
    in
a loving world

A hostile
  person lives
    in
  a hostile world.

Everyone you meet
is your mirror.

KEN KEYES, JR
Handbook to Higher Consciousness

I do not expect anything
from others,
So their actions
cannot be in opposition
to wishes of mine.

SWAMI SRI YUKTESWAR
Autobiography of a Yogi

There are
always risks
in freedom.

The only risk
in bondage
is that
of breaking free.

GITA BELLIN

Be not the slave of your own past—
plunge into the sublime seas,
    dive deep, and swim far,
    so you shall come back
        with self-respect,
        with new power,
        with an advanced experience,
            that shall explain
                and overlook
                    the old.

RALPH WALDO EMERSON

Life is difficult.

This is a great truth,
one of the greatest truths.
It is a great truth because
once we truly see this truth,
we transcend it.

Once we truly know that
life is difficult - once we truly
understand and accept it -
then life is no longer difficult.

Because once it is accepted,
the fact that life is difficult
no longer matters.

M. SCOTT PECK
The Road Less Travelled

The measure of mental health
is the disposition to find good
everywhere.

RALPH WALDO EMERSON

I want to beseech you...
to be patient toward all
that is unsolved in your heart
and try to love the
questions themselves
like locked rooms and
like books
that are written in a
very foreign tongue.

Do not now seek the answers.

which cannot be given you
because you would not be
able to live them.

And the point is, to
live everything.
Live the questions now.

Perhaps you will then
gradually, without noticing it,
evolve some distant day
into the answer.

RAINER MARIA RILKE
Letters to a Young Poet

Have you learned lessons only
   of those who admired you,
   and were tender with you,
   and stood aside for you?

Have you not learned
   great lessons
   from those who braced
   themselves against you,
   and disputed the passage
   with you?

WALT WHITMAN
Leaves of Grass

Rest satisfied with doing well,
and
leave others to talk of you
as they will.

PYTHAGORAS

When some misfortune threatens,
   consider seriously and deliberately
      what is the very worst
         that could possibly happen.

   Having looked this
      possible misfortune in the face,
         give yourself sound reasons
            for thinking that after all
it would be no such terrible disaster.

   Such reasons always exist,
      since at the worst
nothing that happens to oneself
   has any cosmic importance.

When you have looked for some time
steadily at the worst possibility
and have said to yourself
with real conviction "Well, after all,
that would not matter so very much"
you will find that your worry diminishes
to a quite extraordinary extent.

It may be necessary
to repeat the process a few times,
but in the end, if you have
shirked nothing in facing
the worst possible issue,
you will find that
your worry disappears altogether
and is replaced by a kind of
exhilaration.

BERTRAND RUSSELL
The Conquest of Happiness

Be very very still
and allow every new experience
to take place in your life
without any resistance
whatsoever.

You do not have to do anything,
you simply have to be
and let things happen.

EILEEN CADDY
Footprints on the Path

Experience
is determined by yourself -

not the circumstances
of your life.

GITA BELLIN

If you shut your door
        to all errors
truth will be
            shut out.

RABINDRANATH TAGORE

Learn to be silent.

Let your
 quiet mind
  listen
   and absorb.

PYTHAGORAS

Set your sights high,
    the higher the better.

Expect the most wonderful things
    to happen, not in the future
    but right now.

Realise that nothing is too good.

Allow absolutely nothing
    to hamper you
        or hold you up
            in any way.

EILEEN CADDY
Footprints on the Path

Do not be desirous of having
things done quickly. Do not
look at small advantages.
Desire to have things done
quickly prevents their being
done thoroughly. Looking
at small advantages prevents
great affairs from being
accomplished.

CONFUCIUS

You must love yourself
   before you love another.

By accepting yourself
and joyfully
being what you are,
   you fulfill your own abilities,
      and your simple presence
      can make
         others happy.

JANE ROBERTS
The Nature of Personal Reali

Of a certainty
the man who can see
all creatures in himself,
himself in all creatures,
knows no sorrow.

EESHA UPANISHAD

The only successful manifestation
is one which brings about a change
or growth in consciousness:
   that is, it has manifested God,
    or revealed him more fully,
     as well as having
       manifested a form...

DAVID SPANGLER
Manifestation

Ideas by themselves
  cannot produce change of being;
your effort must go in the
  right direction,
    and one must correspond
    to the other.

P. D. OUSPENSKY

Justice is not postponed.
A perfect equity adjusts its
balance in all parts of life.
The dice of God are
always loaded.

The world looks like a
 multiplication table,
 or a mathematical equation,
which, turn it how you will,
balances itself.

Take what figure you will,
its exact value,
nor more or less,
still returns to you.

Every secret is told,
every crime is punished,
every virtue is rewarded,
every wrong redressed,

   in silence and certainty.

RALPH WALDO EMERSON
The Oversoul

Success is a journey
not a destination -
half the fun is getting there.

GITA BELLIN

Never be afraid
  to tread the path alone.

Know which is your path
  and follow it wherever
  it may lead you;

do not feel you have to follow
  in someone else's
        footsteps.

EILEEN CADDY
Footprints on the Path

He who would know the world
seek first
within his being's depths;

He who would truly
know himself
develop interest in the world.

RUDOLF STEINER
How to Know Higher Worlds

The tragedy of a man's life is
what dies inside of him
while he lives.

HENRY DAVID THOREAU

*If one desires a change,
one must be that change
before that change
can take place.*

GITA BELLIN

What things soever ye desire,
when ye pray,
believe that ye receive them,
and ye shall have them.

MARK 11:24

Each player must accept the cards
life deals him or her.

But once they are in hand,
he or she alone must decide
how to play the cards
in order to win the game.

VOLTAIRE

As a progressive and evolving
  being,
man is where he is
  that he may learn
  that he may grow;

  and as he learns the
    spiritual lesson
  which any circumstance
  contains for him

  it passes away
      to other circumstances.

JAMES ALLEN
As a Man Thinketh

Everytime we say
"I must do something"
it takes an incredible
amount of energy.

Far more
than physically
doing it.

GITA BELLIN

Begin with the possible:
begin with one step.
There is always a limit,
you cannot do more than you can.
If you try to do too much,
you will do nothing.

P.D. OUSPENSKY &
G.I. GURDJIEFF

All the world's a stage,
And all the men and women,
     merely players;
They have their exits
     and their entrances,
And one man in his time
     plays many parts.

SHAKESPEARE
As You Like It

*You are never asked
to do more than you are able
without being given
the strength and ability
to do it.*

EILEEN CADDY
The Dawn of Change

God picks up the reed-flute
world and blows.

Each note is a need coming
through one of us,
a passion,
a longing pain.

Remember the lips
where the wind-breath
originated,
and let your note be clear.
Don't try to end it.
Be your note.

I'll show you how it's enough.
Go up on the roof at night.
in this city of the soul.
Let everyone climb on their roofs
and sing their notes!

Sing loud!

RUMI

When one realises
one is asleep.
at that moment
one is already half-awake.

P.D. OUSPENSKY

To find yourself,

Think for yourself.

SOCRATES

You will have
wonderful surges forward.
Then there must be
a time of consolidating
before the next forward surge.

Accept this
as part of the process
and never become
downhearted.

EILEEN CADDY
God Spoke to Me

Doubt is a pain
too lonely to know
that faith
is his twin brother.

KAHLIL GIBRAN
The Prophet

All the powers of your inner Self
are set into activation as a result of
your conscious beliefs. You have lost
a sense of responsibility for your
conscious thought because you have
been taught that it is not what forms
your life. You have been told that
regardless of your belief you are
terrorized by unconscious conditioning.
Some of your beliefs originated in
your childhood, but you are not at
their mercy unless you <u>believe</u> that
you are.

JANE ROBERTS
The Nature of Personal Reality

Life has a bright side and a dark side,
for the world of relativity
is composed of light and shadows.

If you permit your thoughts
to dwell on evil,
you yourself will become ugly.

Look only for the good
in everything,
that you absorb
the quality of beauty.

PARAMAHANSA YOGANANDA
Sayings of Paramahansa Yogananda

Just look next time you are
having some trip and riding
a problem - just watch. Just
stand aside and look at the
problem. Is it really there?
Or have you created it?

Look deeply into it, and you will
suddenly see it is not increasing,
it is decreasing; it is becoming
smaller and smaller.

The more you put your energy
into observation, the smaller it
becomes. And a moment comes
when suddenly it is not there...
you will have a good laugh.

BHAGWAN SHREE RAJNEESH
The Tantra Vision Vol I

A thing is complete
when you can
let it
be.

GITA BELLIN

Cease trying
    to work everything out
        with your minds,
            it will get you nowhere.

Live by intuition
    and inspiration
        and let your whole life
            be a Revelation.

EILEEN CADDY
Footprints on the Path

You will decide
on a matter,
and it will be
established for you,
and light will shine
on your ways.

JOB 22:28

Love alone can unite living beings
so as to complete and fulfill them...
for it alone joins them
by what is deepest
in themselves.

All we need is to imagine
our ability to love developing
until it embraces
the totality of men
and of the earth.

TEILHARD DE CHARDIN

*Forgiveness recognises
what you thought
your brother did to you
has not occurred.*

A COURSE IN MIRACLES

Your subconscious mind
has the answer.

If you are confronted with a problem
and you cannot see
an immediate answer,
assume that your subconscious
has the solution and is
waiting to reveal it to you.

If an answer does not come,
turn the problem over to
your deeper mind prior to sleep.
Keep on turning your request
over to your subconscious until
the answer comes.

The response will be a certain 'feeling,'
an inner awareness,
whereby you 'know' what to do.
Guidance in all things
comes as the still small voice
within:

It reveals all.

BRIAN ADAMS
How to Succeed

If you would learn
  the secret
      of right relations
look only for the divine
      in people and things,
  and leave all the rest to God.

J. ALLEN BOONE
Kinship with all Life

Realise that you cannot
help a soul unless that soul
really wants help and is
ready to be helped.

I tell you to send that soul
nothing but Love and more Love.

Be still and wait,
but be there when that soul
turns for help.

EILEEN CADDY
God Spoke to Me

Men are disturbed not
        by things that happen
but by their opinion of
        the things that happen.

EPICTETUS

You shall be free indeed when
your days are not without a care
nor your nights without a
    want and a grief.

But rather
when these things girdle your life
and yet you rise above them
        naked and unbound.

KAHLIL GIBRAN

We learn wisdom from failure
much more than from success;
we often discover what will do,
by finding out what will not do;
and probably he who
never made a mistake
never made a discovery.

SAMUEL SMILES

Self-knowledge
and self-improvement
are very difficult for most people.

*It usually needs great courage
and long struggle.*

ABRAHAM MASLOW

By going along with feelings,
   you unify
      your emotional,
      mental,
         and bodily states.

When you try to fight
   or deny them,
you divorce yourself
from the reality of your being.

JANE ROBERTS
The Nature of Personal Reality

That which oppresses me,
   is it my soul
   trying to come
   out in the open,
or the soul of the world
knocking at my heart
for its entrance ?

RABINDRANATH TAGORE

Stride forward
  with a firm, steady step
  knowing with
    a deep, certain
        inner knowing
that you will reach
every goal you set yourselves,
that you will achieve
        every aim.

EILEEN CADDY
Footprints on the Path

Be outrageous!

   People who
achieve mastery
have the ability
to be outrageous.

GITA BELLIN

*You should always
be aware that your
head creates
your world.*

KEN KEYES, JR
Handbook to Higher Consciousness

A man must elevate himself
   by his own mind,
   not degrade himself.

The mind is the friend
   of the conditioned soul,
   and his enemy as well.

BHAGAVAD-GITA VI:5

Every issue,
        belief,
            attitude
                or assumption
    is precisely the issue
    that stands between
you and your relationship
    to another human being;
    and between you
                and yourself.

GITA BELLIN

If you depend on someone
  for your happiness
    you are becoming a slave,
      you are becoming dependent,
        you are creating a bondage.

    And you depend on
      so many people; they all
    become subtle masters,
    they all exploit you in return.

BHAGWAN SHREE RAJNEESH
The Book of the Books Vol. IV

To be
upset
over what
you don't have...

is
to waste
what
you do have.

KEN KEYES, JR
Handbook to Higher Consciousness

Gratitude
   helps you to grow and expand;
   gratitude brings joy
   and laughter into your lives
   and into the lives of all those
               around you.

EILEEN CADDY
The Dawn of Change

There is much to use of nature's way.
It is with you always,
available to you always.

Take time to hear and see
that which is close at hand.

There are forces in you untried.

They are yours to be used
as you find them.

JOHN & LYN ST·CLAIR-THOMAS
Eyes of the Beholder

No soul that aspires
can ever fail to rise ;
no heart that loves
can ever be abandoned.

Difficulties exist only
that in overcoming them
we may grow strong,
and they only who
who have suffered
are able to save.

ANNIE BESANT
Some Difficulties of the Inner Life

Be not heedful of the morrow,
but rather gaze upon today,
for sufficient for today
is the miracle thereof.

Be not overmindful
of yourself when you give
but be mindful of the necessity.
For every giver himself receives from
the Father, and that much more
abundantly.

ANNIE BESANT
Some Difficulties of the Inner Life

Faith is an oasis
in the heart
which will never be reached
by the caravan of
thinking.

KAHLIL GIBRAN
Sand and Foam

See every difficulty
as a challenge,
a stepping stone,
and never be defeated
by anything
or anyone.

EILEEN CADDY
The Dawn of Change

Success depends
on where intention
is.

GITA BELLIN

Suffering only hurts because you
   fear it.

Suffering only hurts because you
   complain about it.

It pursues you only because you
   flee from it.

You must not flee,
   you must not complain,
      you must not fear.

   You must love.

Because you know quite well,
deep within you, that there is
  a single magic,
  a single power,
  a single salvation,
  and a single happiness,
and that is called loving.

Well then, love your suffering.
  Do not resist it,
  do not flee from it.

Taste how sweet it is in its essence,
  give yourself to it,
  do not meet it with aversion.

It is only aversion that hurts,
  nothing else.

HERMAN HESSE

The most difficult thing
   but an essential one
Is to love Life,
   to love it even while one suffers,
   because Life is All.

   Life is God —
      and to love Life
         means to love God.

LEO TOLSTOY

I don't know what your destiny
will be,
    but one thing I know:

the only ones among you
    who will be really happy
are those who have sought
    and found
        how to serve.

ALBERT SCHWEITZER

If we are truly in the
  present moment,
and not being carried away by
our thoughts and fantasies,

then we are in a position to
be free of fate and
available to our destiny.

When we are in the
  present moment,
  our work on Earth begins.

RESHAD FEILD

Deep down, within
the core of our being, lies
a creative power, the capacity
to create what is to be, and the
urge to make unremitting efforts
until we have given it shape in
one way or an other, either
outside ourselves, or within
our own person.

J. W. VON GOETHE
From My Life: Poetry and Tru

A soul without
         a high aim
is like a ship
         without a rudder.

EILEEN CADDY
The Dawn of Change

It is good to have an end
to journey towards,
but it is the journey that matters,
in the end.

URSULA LE GUIN
The Left Hand of Darkness

Oftimes a man,
too distrustful of his strength,
fails to secure what is
rightfully his,
being dragged backward by
a spirit deficient in courage.

PINDAR

To follow, under all circumstances, the highest promptings within you; to be always true to the divine self; to rely upon the inward Light, the inward Voice, and to pursue your purpose with a fearless and restful heart, believing that the future will yield unto you the reward of every thought and effort; knowing that the laws of the universe can never fail, and that your own will come back to you with mathematical exactitude, this is faith and the living of faith.

JAMES ALLEN
As a Man Thinketh

How soon
  will you realise
  that the only thing
  you don't have is
  the direct experience

    that there's
    nothing you need

  that you
  don't have ?

KEN KEYES, JR
Handbook to Higher Consciousness

Be afraid of nothing –
you have within you
all wisdom
all power
all strength
all understanding.

EILEEN CADDY
The Dawn of Change

A changed thought system can reverse cause-and-effect as we have known it. For most of us, this is a very difficult concept to accept, because of our resistance to relinquishing the predictability of our past belief system and to assuming responsibility for our thoughts, feelings and reactions.

Since we always look within before looking out, we can perceive attack outside us only when we have first accepted attack as real within.

GERALD G. JAMPOLSKY
Love is Letting Go of Fear

When you affirm your own
rightness in the universe,
then you co-operate with others easily
and automatically
as part of your own nature.

You, being yourself,
help others
be themselves.

Because you recognise
your own uniqueness
you will not need
to dominate others,
nor cringe before them.

JANE ROBERTS
The Nature of Personal Reality

To hate another is to hate yourself.
We all live within the one Universal Mind.
What we think about another,
we think about ourselves.

If you have an enemy, forgive him now.
Let all bitterness and resentment dissolve.
You owe your fellow man love;
show him love, not hate.

Show charity and goodwill toward others
and it will return to enhance
your own life
in many wonderful ways.

BRIAN ADAMS
How to Succeed

I have often wondered how
every man loves himself more
than all the rest of men,

yet sets less value on his
own opinion of himself
than on the opinion of others.

MARCUS AURELIUS
Meditations

If you're into guilt
you're playing God.
The universe is created
so it's O.K. to make a mistake.

If you feel guilty about
what you have done,
you're saying
it's not O.K.
to make mistakes.

Regrets
can hold you back
and can prevent the most
wonderful things
taking place
in your
lives.

EILEEN CADDY
Footprints on the Path

It is proper to doubt.

Do not be led by holy scriptures,
or by mere logic, or inference, or
by appearances, or by the
authority of religious teachers.

But when you realize that
something is unwholesome
and bad for you, give it up.

And when you realize that
something is wholesome
and good for you, do it.

THE BUDDHA

There is but one cause
        of human failure
            and that is
        man's lack of faith
            in his true Self.

WILLIAM JAMES

What we are today
comes from
our thoughts of yesterday,
and our present thoughts
build our life
of tomorrow:

Our life is the creation of our mind.

THE BUDDHA

The past
    is dead

The future
    is imaginary

Happiness
    can only be

in the Eternal

Now

Moment

KEN KEYES, JR.
Handbook to Higher Consciousness

One cannot conquer the evil in
himself by resisting it...
but by transmuting its energies
into other forms.

The energy that expresses
itself in the form of evil
is the same energy
which expresses itself
in the form of good;
and thus the one may
be transmuted into the other.

CHARLES HENRY MACKINTOSH
I Looked on Life

We can only
Be Here Now
when we accept instantly
our moment-by-moment
emotional experience.

GITA BELLIN

Not judging is another way
of letting go of fear and experiencing
Love.

When we learn not to judge
others – and totally accept them,
and not want to change them –
we can simultaneously learn to
accept ourselves.

GERALD G. JAMPOLSKY
Love is Letting Go of Fear

You find true joy
   and happiness in life
when you give
   and give
      and go on giving
         and never count the cost.

EILEEN CADDY
The Dawn of Change

Giving means extending one's Love with no conditions, no expectations and no boundaries.

Peace of mind occurs, therefore when we put all our attention into giving and have no desire to get anything from, or to change, another person.

The giving motivation leads to a sense of inner peace and joy that is unrelated to time.

GERALD G. JAMPOLSKY
Love is Letting Go of Fear

*Perfect kindness
acts
without thinking
of kindness.*

LAO-TSE

Truth does not change
although
   your perception of it
may vary
   or alter
      drastically.

JOHN & LYN ST·CLAIR THOMAS
Eyes of the Beholder

Everything
I do and say
with anyone
makes a difference.

GITA BELLIN

We are built to conquer environment,
solve problems, achieve goals,
and we find no real satisfaction
or happiness in life
without obstacles to conquer
and goals to achieve.

MAXWELL MALTZ
Psycho-Cybernetics

You must understand the
    whole of life,
not just one little part of it.

That is why you must read,
that is why you must look at
    the skies,
that is why you must sing and
dance, and write poems, and
suffer, and understand,

for all that is life.

KRISHNAMURTI

A person who is not disturbed
by the incessant flow of desires—
that enter like rivers into the
ocean, which is ever being
filled but is always still—
can alone achieve peace,
and not the man who strives
to satisfy such desires.

BHAGAVAD-GITA II: 70

Live
and work
but do not forget to play,
to have fun in life
and really enjoy it.

EILEEN CADDY
The Dawn of Change

People with high self esteem
have it because
they have overcome their failures.

They have been put to
the test of life,
overcome the problems
and grown.

DAVID JANSEN

There is little sense in attempting
to change external conditions,
you must first change inner beliefs
then outer conditions
will change accordingly.

BRIAN ADAMS
How to Succeed

The secret of making
   something work in your lives is,
first of all,
      the deep desire to make it work:

then the faith and belief
   that it can work:

then to hold that clear definite
vision in your consciousness
and see it working out
   step by step,
      without one thought
         of doubt or disbelief.

EILEEN CADDY
Footprints on the Path

The greater
    the emphasis
        upon perfection
the further it recedes.

HARIDAS CHAUDHURI
Mastering the Problems of Living

Man has falsely identified
himself with the pseudo-soul
or ego.
When he transfers his sense
of identity to his true being,
the immortal Soul,
he discovers that
all pain is unreal.
He no longer
can even imagine
the state of suffering.

PARAMAHANSA YOGANANDA
Sayings of Paramahansa Yogananda

You make
  yourself and
  others suffer
  just as much
  when

  you take offense

  as when
  you give offense.

KEN KEYES, JR
Handbook to Higher Consciousness

Difficulties are opportunities
to better things;
they are stepping stones
to greater experience.

Perhaps someday
you will be thankful
for some temporary failure
in a particular direction.

When one door closes,
another always opens;
as a natural law it has to,
to balance.

BRIAN ADAMS
How to Succeed

There is no situation that could
ever confront you that cannot be solved.
Life takes on real meaning when
you set values for yourself,
regard yourself as worthwhile
and elevate your thoughts to
things that are of God (good).

There is a Higher Power.
Turn to it and use it;

It is yours for the asking.

BRIAN ADAMS
How to Succeed

Work
    is love
        made visible.

KAHLIL GIBRAN
The Prophet

It is important
    from time to time
    to slow down,
       to go away by yourself,
       and simply
          Be.

EILEEN CADDY
The Dawn of Change

It is within my power either to
   serve God,
   or not to serve Him.

Serving Him,
   I add to my own good and
   the good of the whole world.

Not serving Him,
   I forfeit my own good and
   deprive the world of that good,

which was in my power to create.

LEO TOLSTOY

When a man finds that it is
his destiny to suffer, he will
have to accept his suffering
as his task;
his single and unique task.
He will have to acknowledge
the fact that even in suffering
he is unique and alone in the
Universe.

No one can relieve him of
his suffering or suffer in his
place. His unique opportunity
lies in the way in which he
bears his burden.

VIKTOR FRANKL
Man's Search for Ultimate Meaning

Like attracts like.

Whatever the conscious mind
thinks and believes
the subconscious
identically
creates.

BRIAN ADAMS
How to Succeed

We are injured and hurt emotionally
~ not so much by other people
or what they say or don't say ~
but by our own attitude
and our own response.

MAXWELL MALTZ
Psycho-Cybernetics

A tree that can fill the span
 of a man's arms
 grows from a downy tip;

A terrace nine storeys high
 rises from hodfuls of earth;

A journey of a thousand miles
 starts from beneath one's feet.

LAO-TZU

*Every end
is a new
beginning.*

ACKNOWLEDGEMENTS

Especially I wish to thank Malcolm Cohan for his love, and constant encouragement without which this book would have never been started, sustained or completed. I would like to thank Margo Snape for her beautiful jacket artwork, Shane McCoy for his wonderful illustrations, and Liz Faul for additonal calligraphy. Further, I would like to express my deepest thanks to my family and friends, whose presence in my life contributed, whether directly or indirectly, towards this book. Finally, I would like to acknowledge all the great spirits I have quoted in this book whose words have given so much to my understanding and growth.

I am grateful to the publishers and authors who kindly gave permission to reproduce copyright material from the following:

BRIAN ADAMS, *How to Succeed*, 1985 Melvin Powers Wilshire Book Co, California. J. ALLEN BOONE, *Kinship With All Life*, 1954 Harper & Row New York. GITA BELLIN, *A Sharing Of Completion And Celebration*, 1983 Self-Transformation Seminars Ltd. EILEEN CADDY, *The Dawn of Change*, 1979, *God Spoke To Me* 1971, *Footprints On The Path*, 1976 Findhorn Foundation, Scotland UK. RODNEY COLLIN *The Theory of Conscious Harmony*. Rodney Collin, Janet Collin Smith (Editor) 1998, By The Way Books California. RESHAD FEILD *Steps to Freedom*, 1998 Chalice Guild UK. VIKTOR FRANKL *Man's Search for Ultimate Meaning*. Viktor E. Frankl, Victor Emil Unbewusste Gott Frankl, Viktor Frankl, Swanee Hunt, 1997. Insight Books. SHAKTI GAWAIN, *Creative Visualisation*, 1978 Whatever Publishing Inc., California. HARIDAS CHAUDHURI, *Mastering The Problems of Living*, 1968. Theosophical Publishing House, Illinois. KAHLIL GIBRAN *Sand and Foam*, 1926, *Jesus The Son of Man*, 1928, *The Prophet* 1923 © Kahlil Gibran. Source Material from Alfred A. Knopf, Inc., Random House., New York. VERNON HOWARD, *The Mystic Path To Cosmic Power*, 1976. Parker Publishing Company, Inc. GERALD G. JAMPOLSKY, *Love Is Letting Go Of Fear*, 1979. G. Jampolsky and Jack O. Keeler, Celestial Arts, California. KEN KEYES, JR. *Handbook To Higher Consciousness*, Fifth Edition, 1975. The Living Love Center, Kentucky.

J. KRISHNAMURTI, *Krishnamurti's Journal,* 1982. Krishnamurti Foundation Trust Ltd, Kent, UK. Dr MAXWELL MALTZ, *Psycho-Cybernetics,* 1960 Prentice-Hall, Inc. New Jersey. ABRAHAM H. MASLOW, T*oward a Psychology of Being* Abraham H. Maslow, Richard Lowry, 1998. John Wiley & Sons. NISAMI *The Haft Paykar: A Medieval Persian Romance,* 1995. Julie Scott Meisami (Translator), Ganjavi Nizami Oxford University Press. BHAGWAN SHREE RAJNEESH, (now known as OSHO) *Dying for Enlightenment* 1979, *The Sacred Yes* 1983, *The Book Of The Books Vol. IV* 1976, *The Sound Of One Hand Clapping* 1981, *Walking In Zen, Sitting In Zen* 1982, *A Cup Of Tea* 1980, *The Goose Is Out* 1982, *The Tantra Vision Vol 1* 1978. JANE ROBERTS, *The Nature Of Personal Reality,* 1974. Prentice-Hall Inc., New Jersey. M.SCOTT PECK *The Road Less Traveled*: A New Psychology of Love, Traditional Values and Spiritual Growth, 1998. Simon & Schuster N.Y. BERTRAND RUSSEL, *The Conquest of Happiness,* 1975 George Allen & Unwin Publishers Ltd. RAINER MARIA RILKE *Letters to a young poet.* (Classic Wisdom Collection 1992) New World Library. RUMI *The Essential Rumi* by Jelalludin Rumi, Coleman Barks (Translator), John Moyne (Translator), A. Arberry, 1997. Book Sales USA. JOHN & LYN ST. CLAIR-THOMAS, *Eyes Of The Beholder,* 1982. John & Lyn St Clair-Thomas & Steven Shackel. Angel Publications, Australia. Dr RABINDRANATH TAGORE, *Glorious Thoughts Of Tagore,* 1965 New Book Society of India. *Collected Poems & Plays Of Rabindranath Tagore* 1936 Macmillan, London & Basingstoke, UK. Dr DENIS WAITLEY, *The Winners Edge,* 1980. Times Books, New York. PARAMAHANSA YOGANANDA, *Autobiography Of A Yogi* 1946. Copyright newewed 1974 by Self-Realization Fellowship, California. *Spiritual Diary,* 1968. Self-Realization Fellowship, California. A COURSE IN MIRACLES 1975. Foundation For Inner Peace. Inc.

Every effort has been made to ensure each author is properly acknowledged, although some sources were not traced. Please contact the publisher for any errors or omissions.